Where I Live

A first geography book for young children in the Harrisburg, Pennsylvania area.

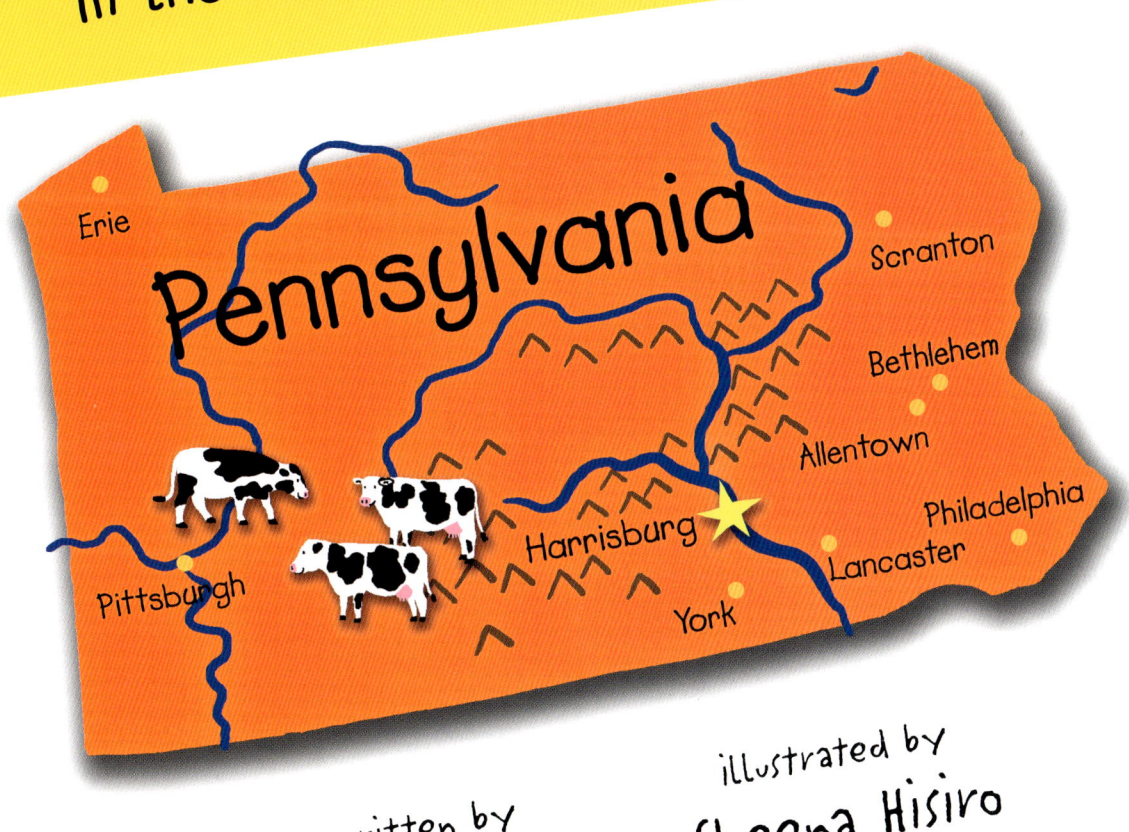

written by
Debra Hervitz

illustrated by
Sheena Hisiro

This book is dedicated to all my wonderful students, past, present and future. A special thank you goes to Floyd Stokes, Sheena Hisiro, my mother, husband, and children for believing in me.

- d.h.

To Gramma and Pap

- s.h.

No part of this publication may be reproduced in whole or part, or stored on a retrieving system, or transmitted in any form or by any means, electronic, mechanical, photocopying, recording, or otherwise, without written permission of the publisher. For more information regarding permission, contact debrahervitz@whereilivebook.com

Text copyright © 2013 by Debra Hervitz.
Illustrations copyright © 2014 by Sheena Hisiro.
Graphic Design by Sheena Hisiro.
First Edition, 2015. Second Edition, 2015.
Third Edition, 2016. Fourth Edition, 2017.
All rights reserved.

ISBN 978-0-09960857-0-0

PRINTED IN CHINA

Children need to know where they live as well as the vocabulary for describing these places. Reading this book and discussing its contents will give children this opportunity and open their minds to a whole new world.

"There is no place like home, but oh the places you'll go!"

-Debra Hervitz
Certified Reading Specialist

Mars

Earth

The sun is a star.

Venus

Mercury

I am up in a rocket ship and I can see the eight planets in our <u>solar system</u>. Their names are Mercury, Venus, Earth, Mars, Jupiter, Saturn, Uranus, and Neptune.

Jupiter

Saturn

Uranus

Neptune

Sun

I live on the planet Earth.

Moon

North
West East
South

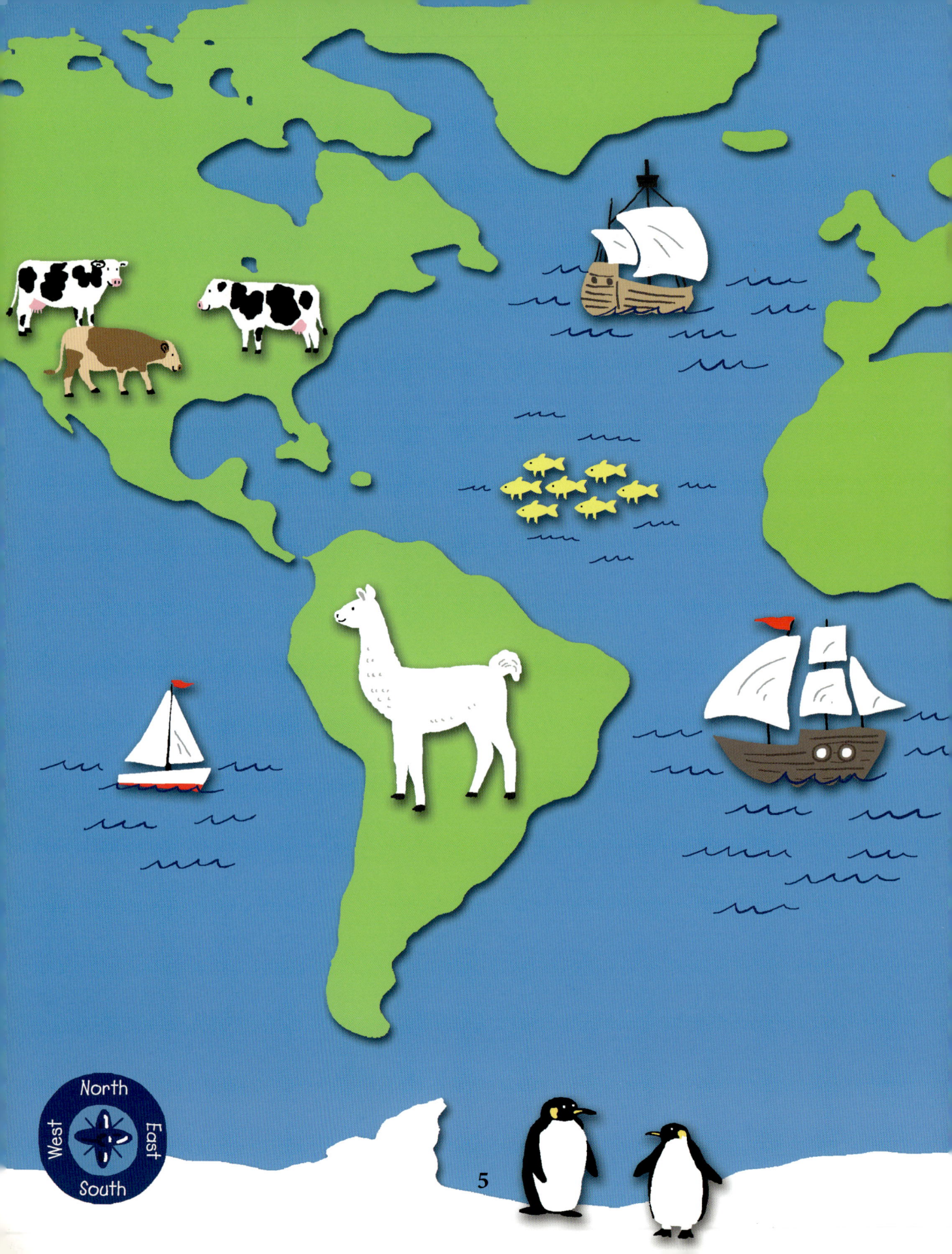

5

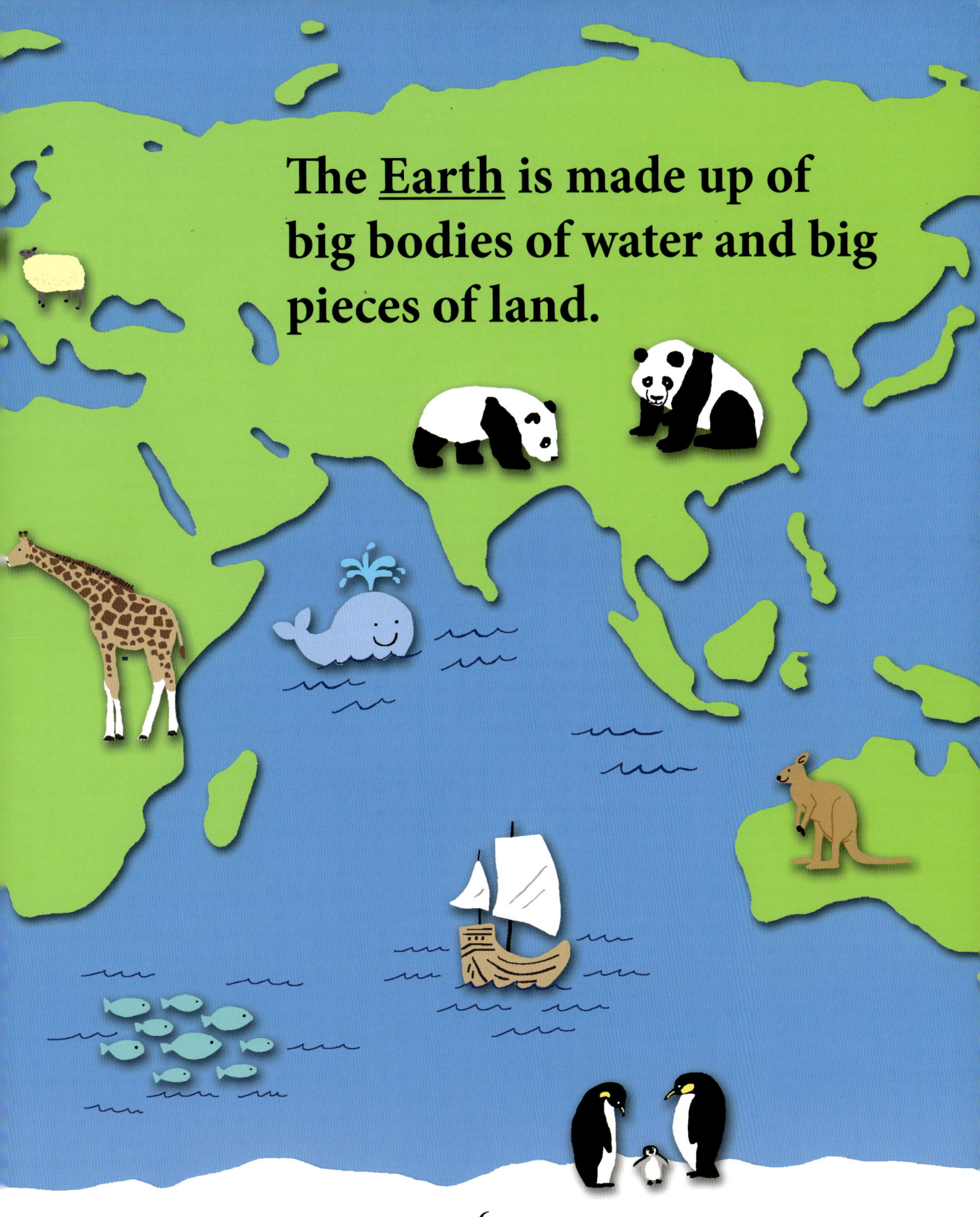

The **Earth** is made up of big bodies of water and big pieces of land.

The big bodies of water are called <u>oceans</u>. There are four oceans. They are Atlantic, Pacific, Arctic and Indian.

"Ocean Song"
(Sing to My Bonnie Lies Over the Ocean)

Atlantic is one of our oceans
Pacific and Indian too!
The Arctic is often forgotten.
I'll try to remember, won't you.

Atlantic, Pacific, Arctic
and Indian too.
Earths four oceans, I'll try
to remember, won't you.

The big pieces of land are called <u>continents</u>. There are seven continents.

North America

Europe

Africa

South America

Antarctica

The names of the continents are Asia, Africa, North America and South America, Europe, Australia, and Antarctica.

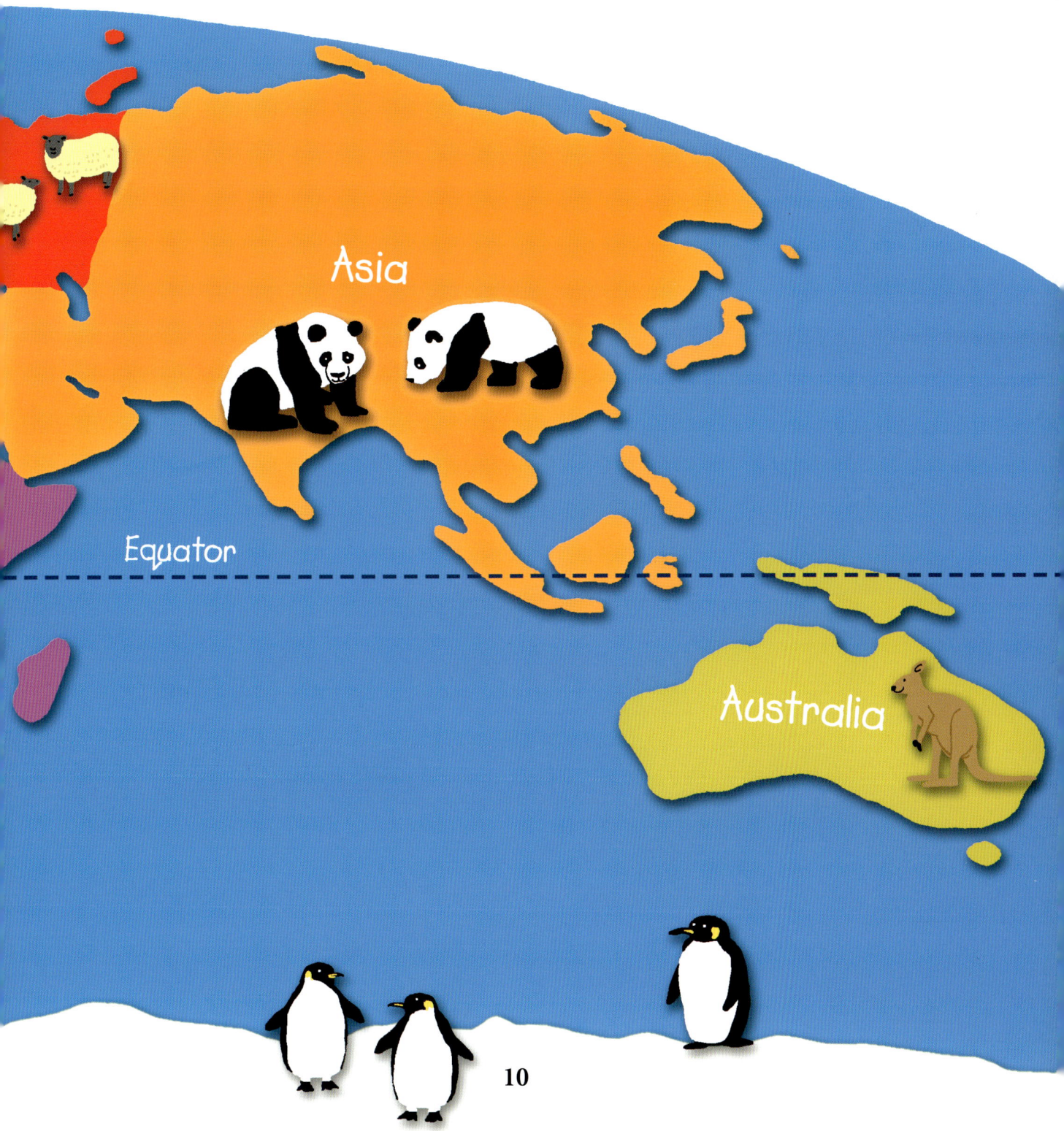

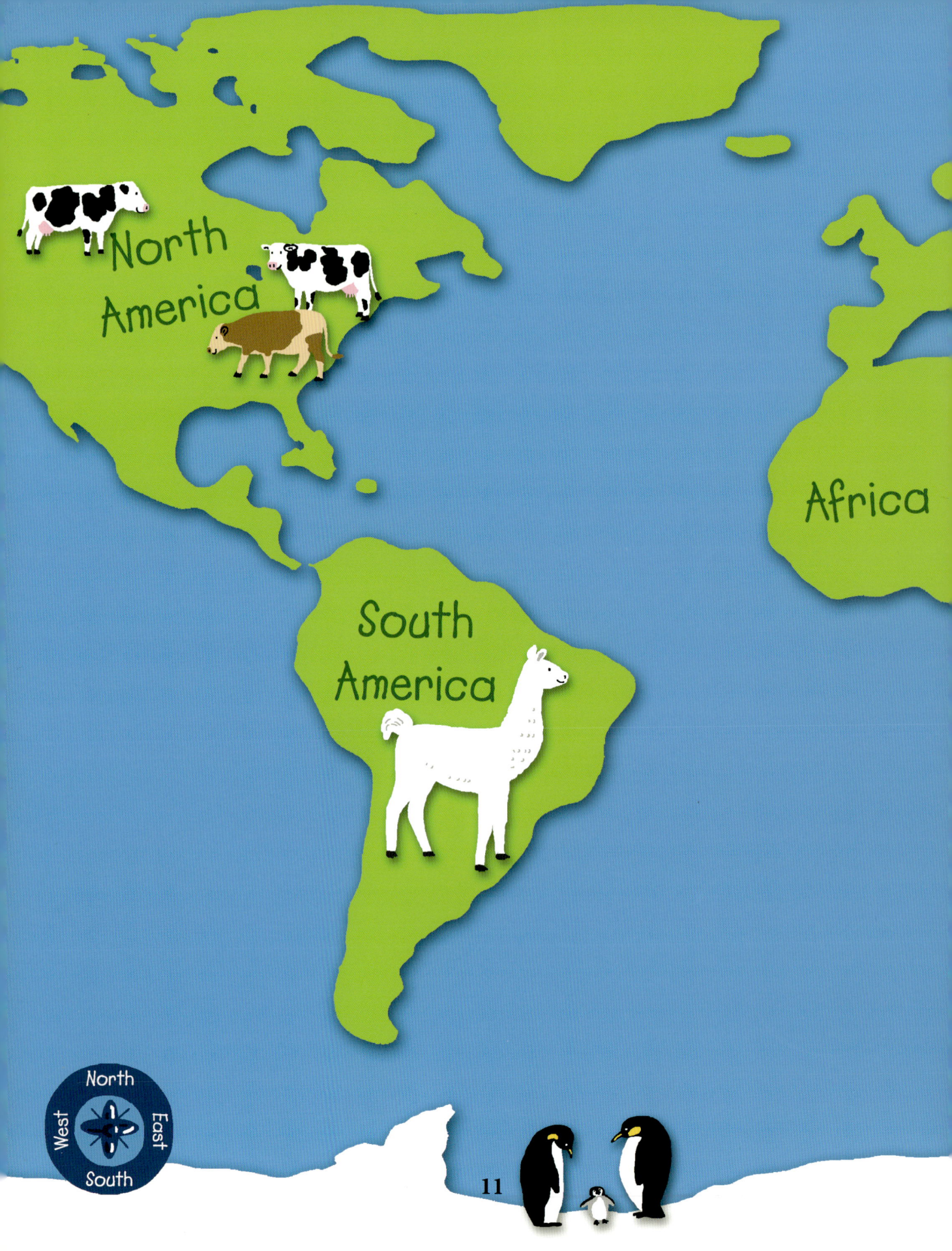

North America

South America

Africa

North
West ✦ East
South

11

"The Continent Song"
(Sing to Mary Had a Little Lamb)

There are seven continents,
continents, continents.
There are seven continents,
on the planet Earth.

Australia, Antarctica,
Asia, Africa,
North and South America,
and Europe too!

Europe

Asia

Australia

Antarctica

Pacific Ocean

North America

Harrisburg

North
West East
South

I live on the continent of **North America.**

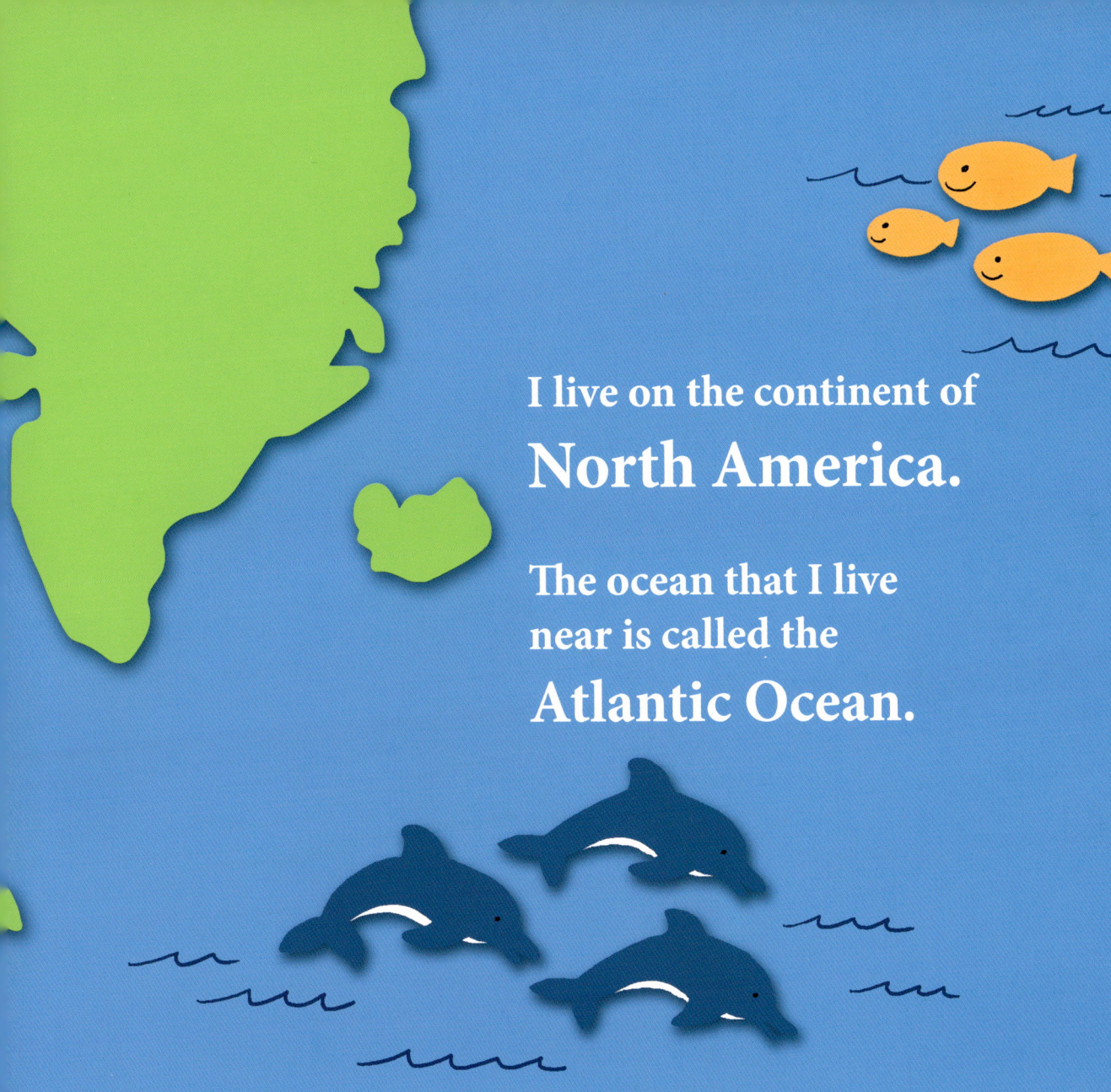

The ocean that I live near is called the **Atlantic Ocean.**

Atlantic Ocean

14

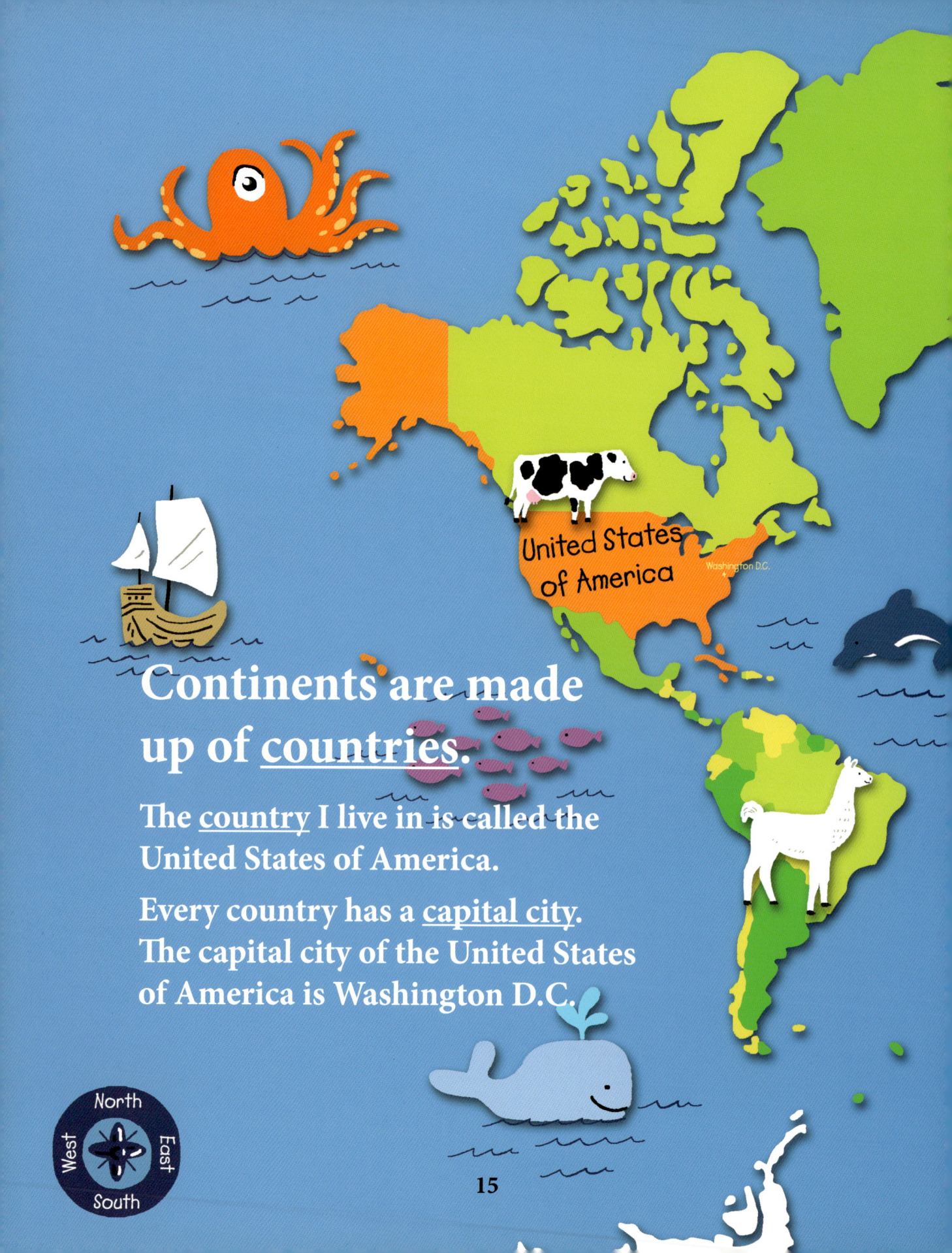

Continents are made up of countries.

The country I live in is called the United States of America.

Every country has a capital city. The capital city of the United States of America is Washington D.C.

16

Washington
Montana
North Dakota
Oregon
Idaho
South Dakota
Wyoming
Nebraska
Nevada
Utah
Colorado
California
Kansas
Oklahoma
Arizona
New Mexico
Texas
Alaska
Hawaii

North
West East
South

17

The United States of America is made up of 50 **states**. I live in the state of Pennsylvania.

Every state has a **capital city**. The capital city of Pennsylvania is Harrisburg.

Pennsylvania

Lake Erie

New York

Erie

Scranton

Bethlehem

Allentown

Philadelphia

Pittsburgh

Harrisburg

Lancaster

York

Ohio

Maryland

Delaware

West Virginia

Virginia

North, South, East, West

19

Massachusetts

Connecticut

Rhode Island

Atlantic Ocean

States are made up of many <u>counties</u>. The <u>county</u> I live in is called _____ County.

Counties are made up of many <u>cities</u>, <u>townships</u> and <u>boroughs</u>. Some people live in the city of Harrisburg or in an area near Harrisburg. What is the name of your city, township or borough?

Harrisburg Area

1. Capitol Building
2. Civil War Museum
3. The State Museum of Pennsylvania
4. Fort Hunter
5. Hershey Park

📖 Libraries

The Harrisburg area has a large <u>river</u> that runs through it. It is called the Susquehanna River.

Interstate 81

Enola

Route 11
Lemoyr
Camp Hill
Carlisle Pike
Carlisle
PA Route 581
Route 15

North / West / East / South

Mechanicsburg

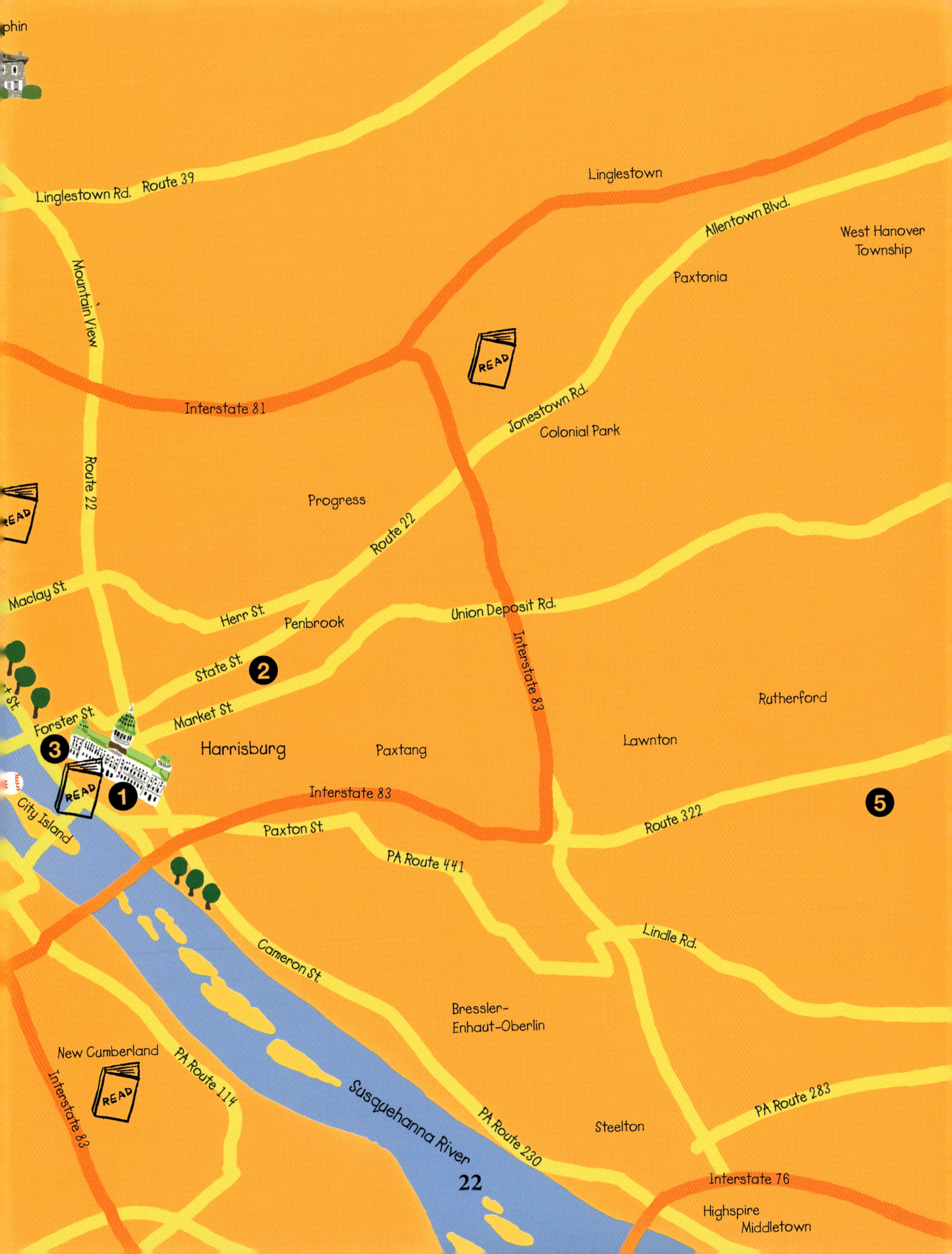

There are many streets in the Harrisburg area. The number on my home and the street on which I live is called my <u>address</u>.

Now I am home. What a fun trip! Here is a picture of my home.

(Draw a picture of your house)

Geography Games

These fun and educational games help children to acquire knowledge of places around the world. This is a useful way for children to read maps and globes.

Game #1
The object of this game is to name places that begin with the last letter of the place previously stated.

How to Play:
One person is selected to choose a name of a place. It can be a name of a river, ocean, city, state, country, continent or planet. The next person must name another place that begins with the last letter of that place. Players are eliminated when they are unable to name a place. The last person remaining is the winner.

Game #2
The object of this game is to name places in the world that touch, or border, one another.

How to Play:
The first player names a place. If the first player names Pennsylvania, the second would name Ohio or Maryland. The game can continue in either of two ways:
1. The next person names the next place that is connected, such as Delaware, or
2. He can choose any other place on the planet to which the other player must respond with a connected location.

These geography games can be utilized with the help of maps or globes.

Enjoy these games at school or at home with your family!

All About Me

My **name** is _____.
　　　　　　　　　First　　　　　　　　　_Last_

My **address** is _____.
　　　　　　　　　Number　_Street_　　_City_　　　_State_

I live in the **county** of _____.

I live in or near the **city** of _____.

The **state** I live in is called _____.

The **country** I live in is called _____.

The **continent** I live in is called _____.

The **planet** I live on is called _____.

I live near the _____ **Ocean**.

The **river** that flows through Harrisburg area is called the

_____ **River**.